Emotional Malaise Syndrome

by W. Allen, Phd.

DORRANCE
PUBLISHING CO
EST. 1920
PITTSBURGH, PENNSYLVANIA 15238

RoseDog Books
585 Alpha Drive
Suite 103
Pittsburgh, PA 15238
Visit our website at www.rosedogbookstore.com

ISBN: 978-1-4809-8022-8
eISBN: 978-1-4809-8045-7

A Little light
This can be a wonderful place to write
Perhaps on into the late night
All I need is a little light

W. Allen 10-3-1972

Table of Contents

Disclaimer

The psychosocial focus of this article is the effects of a particular way of interacting; that can cause emotional suffering (emotional malaise). This article does not purport to cure the symptoms of emotional malaise. Any one can experience an "emotional malaise (EM)." EM has many faces (causes)! One type may with in reason usually remit over time (usually if there are no presenting Psychostenia* or medical indications, etcetera); which is usually accomplished if the sufferer become aware of their plight an act upon it, or with the help of a friend, parent(s), a professional, or literally any one who can explaining/expose the dynamics that empower an malaise phenomena.

Note! Any one can unknowingly experience such symptoms and not be consciously aware of "why." The other particular face of emotional malaise

presented here, which is its main focus, is of a more emotionally disturbing type! "It maybe characterized by some of the following symptoms, such as inhibited cognitive functioning, doubt, blame, feelings of guilt, fault, lack of confidence, in ability to reach goals aspired to, as well as difficultly interacting with others, an may also experience difficulty attending to the challenges of daily living, etcetera." Remission may be difficul to achieve. It does not purport to be a cure, treatment, or at this time attempt to create an additional diagnostic category to added to the present cadre of mental disorders; But, it does examine some of the dynamics of an actor, who may interact with others in such a way, as to cause them to experience some of the emotional symptoms mention above -thereby possibly causing them to suffer an EM. "Otherwise, it encourages one to seek help (professional or otherwise) if indicated; an to exposes an brings attention/awareness to a phenomena; that has literally existed for eons; unnoticed affecting untold multitudes of persons in relationships; under the radar of our collective conscious awareness; in the interim suffers may become just another casualty or remain guilt ridden an baffled; as concerned on lookers/others may be unable/willing to help; primarily, due to a lack of understanding of how to approach the presentation of symptoms of this phenomena, etcetera."

Preface

This article explores the effect of interpersonal interaction relationship(s); actor vs. recipient respectively; that can cause the latter to suffer various symptoms of an emotional malaise. "As mention in the disclaimer; it attempts to exposes an brings attention/awareness to a phenomena; that has literally existed for eons (unnoticed affecting untold numbers of persons in relationships) under the radar of our collective conscious awareness; while suffers may become just another casualty or remain guilt ridden an baffled; as concerned others may be unable or unwilling to help; due to a lack of understanding of how to approach the phenomena, etcetera."

The article attempts to further point out there are numerous reasons for the cause of an emotional malaise; an here we call attention to at least two types of emotional malaises (there are many due to other related causes). "The first one is a rather benign type; as a person's reaction/response to such a situation maybe characterized as within the norm/common; as one become aware of the effect it has had on them; the symptoms will usually remit when attended to!" The symptoms will usually remit; as they maybe "benign" episodes; that may also be characterized as being situational, temporary, transitory, contingent, etcetera.

"The second one of concern is a more toxic/malignant type." It can be characterized by inhibited emotional suffering, leaving one unable to attend to the daily challenges of life, as well as an inability to attain desires goals an aspirations, etcetera. This is a more severe form of EM, that is not so easily resolved-by explanation. Relief is not so antidotal. The symptoms maybe emotionally debilitating an unremitting; impacting (subconsciously) on one's ability to function at a particular/desired level. Subsequently, you are not functioning normally, an do not consciously knowing why. The answer may be related to the effects of interaction(s) in relationship(s); which may inhibit the attainment of desired goals, etcetera.

"The second one of concern is a more toxic/malignant type." It can be characterized by inhibited emotional suffering, leaving one unable to attend to the daily challenges of life, as well as an inability to attain desires goals an aspirations, etcetera. This is a more severe form of EM, that is not so easily resolved-by explanation. Relief is not so antidotal. The symptoms maybe emotionally inhibiting an unremitting; impacting (subconsciously) on one's ability to function at a particular/desired level. Subsequently, you are not as mention if indicated functioning normally, an do not consciously knowing why. The answer may be related to interaction(s) in relationship(s); which may inhibit the attainment of desired goals, etcetera.

There is no claim here to cure emotional malaise. However, the question is asked, "if you are suffering from a malaise?" If so then you should consider seeking professional services or that of others in examples.

Beyond that it strives to describe the dynamics of a would be nemesis -an actor(s) in your life; as well as helpful suggestions on what to consider when becoming involved in a relationship (intimate, formal, etcetera); an getting help (professionals or otherwise) where indicated. It also call attention to this phenomena of interacting in a certain/particular way; that can cause another to suffer an EM (characterized by symptoms mention in this article); which appear inadvertently hidden from our collective conscious awareness for eons.

Furthermore, if was mention that some of the expectations of our intuitions (etcetera), should be examined for alternatives to help support aforementioned types of failed relations . It is not a formula for treatment, or claim to be a diagnosis for any mental disorder. However, it recommend if you are in a toxic/malignant relationship; that may be characterized by some of the symptoms mention in this article -going forward; that you should consider seeking professional services/etcetera if indicated...

Dedication

For those who have or remain in inequitable relationships an may suffer an not consciously know why! Through your interactions with your partner/actor, for what ever reason or not, You may have been condition to feel all of the difficulties in your relationship are your fault/blame/etcetera. Subsequently you are bound up in the dynamics of an emotional malaise; with the tragedy being you feel hopeless. It can be debilitating an literally drain your psychic energy; that might have helped motivated you to even question your condition in the relationship -let alone attempt to challenge it.

Furthermore, this dedication is for persons (recipients) who may not consciously be aware that they have become victimized by others (actors); as they interact with them who say what they will/to get what they want. "If what they say is what you subconsciously want to hear/or except; an you do not at least question (the who, what, when, were, why, an how) the actor's motivation; then following that you may form a questionable bond, vow, etc." "However, if afterwards there are repeated episodes of verbal (exploitation) an or physical abuse, attempts at casting blame, doubt, minimizing you, unfairness, an promise or broken vows not kept; you then return repeatedly or remain in the relationship; then you may subconsciously becoming part of the dynamics of an EM." Some of the "tell tale" symptoms of an EM are described in the aforegoing article; which aspires to motivate suffers to seek appropriate help care services -where indicated… Otherwise, the alternative may be a condition, that may bind you to an exploitive none productive relationship -for an indeterminate period of time…

About the author

The author is a Board Certified licensed clinical psychotherapist; earned several degrees in social science; as well as degrees in counseling and clinical psychology. The author also studied metaphysical healing, an applied psychology, has earned over 30> yrs of post continuing education credits (CEU) involving current related topics. The author's work history involves working in a Regional Medical Center Hospital in the Mental Health Complex; working as a clinical coordinator in a community outreach mental health clinic; also during those times concurrently maintained a private practice; as well as working in community center(s), CPS, family services, an also related court work several time per week...

During that time the author developed an interest in the effects of interaction in interpersonal relationship on others; as illustrated in (Scared Affair) a "fictitious" account of a character (actor) exploiting others for his own selfish ends; as the victims were not consciously aware of their motives which may have allowed themselves to be exploited. They may have been in denial, not consciously aware that they were being exploited; an may have desperately "needed" to believe what was said/promised, etcetera. It also illustrated the gullibility of others in relationships; who unwittingly/ unknowingly allow themselves to be treated in such worthless ways; as they appeared to have valued the relationship more that their own convictions/ standards/morals, etc). "Although it was a factious entertaining novel; it illustrated how people become victimized; an may not know how or why. It further attempts to illustrate the power of the dynamics in such relationships; that would have otherwise remained under the radar of our collective awareness.

The author's thesis /book on the (Effects of Mathophobia on Career Choice 1983) further illustrated the effects of interaction initiated by actors; that may be a critical cause of a recipient to suffer symptoms of an emotional malaise; related to making a career choice.

Considering the author's experience (involving work an literary history as well as academics, and research) an opinion evolves that suggest; there is a dire need in the health care industry/field; for professionals to become more aware of those suffering (EM) with out hope; an not consciously knowing why - endlessly suffer such effects.

To help alleviate some of the suffering from symptoms of EM (less you be deterred); it is imperative that one keep in mind; that the processing of an individual to this particular emotional state; is literally so subtle an lacking in awareness of the part of the individual; that the victim(s) do not usually complain. Also remember there is a massive invisible population of suffers who need relief from the negative effects of particular interpersonal relationships; who in the author's opinion some appeared to have resolutely existed in "zombie like states" over an indeterminate period of time; impervious of their condition/status in their relationship with no conscious desire/motivation to change.

"During the author's years of work; a quantity of knowledge an experience were acquired; it became focused on numerous relationships that appeared to be predatory relationships renascent /related to their interpersonal relationship with an actor(s) or others; that appeared to have rendered them (recipient) to such a state (malaise); that they were literally sapped of their psychic energy; to the point that they did not have enough will power/energy or desire to escape their situation; as they were unable/unwilling to think objectively of there situation an remove/escape its influence(s)." ,

"Furthermore, in the author's opinion these particular kind of relationships referred to exist; when it renders the other (recipient) in the relationship to suffer an emotional malaise; which affect them cognitively (as they may not be able to think clearly/logically); an subsequently they feel they are the blame for all that is "wrong" in their relationship(s). Furthermore, they also experience feelings of blame, doubt, lack of confidence, as well as not being able to attain a desired goals, reach or function at their potential/optimum level, etcetera." They may not consciously be aware of the conditioning/process that was foisted upon them by the actor for selfish reasons or otherwise. Note: The actor may not be aware of their motivation either; as they may have some clinical issues that may involve depression, "decompensation", etcetera. "Classic cases maybe described as follows: being overwhelmed by what appeared to be a predatory relationship; where they were Unable/unwilling to improve their lot; related to a lack of conscious awareness that they have been processed into an EM; where as they are not consciously aware they are being manipulated by the kind of interaction that takes place in their relationship; rendering them to thinking their situation is hopeless an all their fault." Also keep in mind awareness is lacking on the part of some laymen as well as professionals respectively; relative to this phenomena an needs to address the same; an research designs are need to further suggest helpful directions. With this in mind, it is the author's opinion as the phenomena is brought to the conscious awareness of others an professionals (with training/education), they may be able to affect some relief for some who are amenable to help/treatment.

Emotional Malaise Sydrome

Chapter One/Emotional Malaise

Are you suffering from an Emotional Malaise? Have you ever found yourself thinking/feeling you have failed as a "personality" (that you have not reach your potential or goals you aspired to)? "They maybe attainable an not beyond your abilities; but, for one reason or another you have not." "Then, perhaps you may be experiencing what is refer to here as an emotional malaise (EM)." "Are you experiencing an emotional malaise?" "Perhaps you may not be aware that you are. It is possible!"

Chapter Two/What is an Emotional Malaise

"In order to understand if you are suffering from an EM, you must first understand what it is!" EM referred to here is not a clinical diagnosis, nor for our purposes here will you find it in a Diagnostic Statistical Manual (DSM). [1] However, in this particular it is being referred to here as a general term alluding to; "when you allow someone into your life, who has such an effect upon you; that it may subconsciously interfere with your cognitive functioning; which may be characterized by appearing to inhibit you from reaching your potential(s); such as a particular contribution, goals, desires, a way of thinking, a certain style of dressing, etcetera, challenges of daily living, or a way of doing things -and so on. You may also feel you're the blame for everything and can do nothing right. Your thinking process maybe literally riddled with doubt an lack of confidence."

"However, Usually after the cause of the above mention symptoms are exposed/examined/explained; the situation may usually be alleviate by several means; such as challenges that may

[1] DSM -5 (2013) Published by the American Psychological Association, NYC, NY.

correct/improve the actor's interactive behavior (verbal/physica behavioral responses), etcetera towards the recipient/YOU; as well as dissolution of a relationship (you previously felt hopelessly bound to); supportive services as well as help from others tolerance, etcetera." If there is no remittance; then the relationship/situation maybe more toxic than realized; an at this point professional service(s) may be indicated; as it may no longer appear to be a benign emotional malaise ...

If you continue to experience these symptoms (suffering); the proceeding may or may not aid in helping you to alleviate the same or make such a determination; as life is complicated an each situation is unique within itself. The proceeding is not a panacea. "What it is does gives some insight into what could possibly cause an EM and some alternatives to address the same." To experience an EM does not necessarily mean you are suffering from a clinical disorder such as depression, or another mental illness of a psychasthenic* nature, etcetera .

But, beyond this point other aspects of the emotional malaise syndrome (EMS) will be addressed and if professional services may be indicated. " If you feel you are suffering an experienced little or no relief from such symptoms, etcetera , then seek a consultation with a competent healthcare professional (etcetera)." Otherwise, the particular EM referred to here presents a phenomena, that has heretofore existed under the radar -literally unnoticed. Furthermore, this presentation of EM is not intended to be a clinical model for treatment; nor has it become a name for a disorder; in the sense that it has passed the rigors of being included in the DSM. [2]

---

[2] DSM -5 (2013) Published by the American Psychological Association, NYC,NY.

To experience episodes of symptoms of EM mentioned above does not necessarily mean you are mentally ill, as this just may be a transitory reaction; as you would responded to particular circumstance(s) in your life. Your malfunctioning usually may not earn you a diagnosis of mental illness. "But, it certainly may be an indication something is not right in your life, an it maybe time to address it accordingly."

The irony/contradiction is you may not necessarily be suffering from a clinical disorder. "But, unknowingly you may not be living up to your desired potential; because of the effects (emotional, etcetera) someone else is causing you to experience." "Or you may feel you are just not reaching your potential an don't consciously know why." "You may feel you are in a situation you can't do anything about or get out of." "You may feel like a "loser." "Or you may just be literally hanging in limbo.." You may possibly be to ashamed to discuss your plight with significant others in your life such as, your mom, dad, other family members, close friends, pastor, or even a stranger, etc. [3]

"However, whomever is having such an influence upon you; you are not consciously allowing them to have such an impact on your life. But, the actor may (or not) be eligible for a clinical diagnosis or worse. An assessment may have to be made by professionals for a determination. Individual/ Couple counseling maybe indicated, etcetera. But, usually you are not aware of the influence they have upon you."

---

*A mental disorder characterized by phobias, obsessions, compulsions, or excessive anxiety. The term is no longer in psychiatric diagnostic use.
DSM -5 (2013) Published by the American Psychological Association, NYC, NY.

[3] Eysenck, Hans, J. (1980a) A Unifying Theory and Spontaneous Rem ission. Zeitschrist Fur Psychologie, 188 (1) 43-56.

Perhaps, you would think the reverse is true! You think of it happening to someone else. However, "it really is happening to you." But, there is no conscious awareness of the process. There is no obvious victim or any one complaining -say except yourself if at all. "Perhaps, in so many words others have tried to tell you." "But, say you just don't want to listen/agree, in denial, or on a conscious level, just don't want to acknowledge it either." "Perhaps, in jest it can almost be comparable to a good old magician's trick!" "Here you have a subject literally being hung. But, to one's surprise the subject in not complaining." In fact upon further examination/observations it would appear they are "really" helping to hang themselves.

Chapter Three/ The Dynamics of your mimesis

Your nemesis's behavior in some instances may literally be characterized as predatory. "Or, your nemesis maybe characterized as someone you're in a relationships with; [4] who as indicated above has a conditioning history or their motivation maybe derived from experienced unresolved emotional conflicts with others; whereby, their verbal interaction with you maybe very subtle (overt or even literally encrypted); or for example coded with key words or behavior; that may elicit a particular(s) emotional/behavioral response(s) from you; an as a result no matter what your response(s) is/are; you may not "seem to have the ability/capacity to interact positively with him/her."

At sometimes in their lives they may have experienced conflicts, that resulted in negative emotional outcomes i.e., involving bonding, love, rejection, verbal abuse, physical abuse, detachment, minimization, a learning experience, etcetera. Subsequently, they may think others feel they are "unimportant!" [5] They may feel they must be the "boss" -to

---

[4] Jones,Dasha, (1996),W hatM en Find Sexy, (Upscale Comm unications Inc),Atlanta,Ga.P 34.

[5] Allen,W (1983)The effects ofM athophobia on CareerChoice Columbia Pacific University, M Ill

compensate... They may further experience feeling of anxiousness, worthlessness, as well as helplessness. The range of experientially negative emotional feelings maybe to numerous to catalogue here. The actor's motivation could stem from one dominate conflict; or they may cycle through a range of their defense mechanism; to attain their desired effect upon you (recipient -or others too when needed).

"When people experience frustration, stress, etcetera they may usually use several modes of communicating with others! These modes (not precluding others) are generally referred to as (1) blaming mode, (2) distracter mode, (3) computer mode, (4) placator mode, and (5) leveler/leveling mode." [6] Person(s) /actor(s) who electively adapt to use the blamer mode may have experienced conflicts as mentioned above! "Subsequently, they struggle in their attempts to interact with others; as they adapt to communicate with others in a blamer mode in an attempt to compensate themselves."

"Or, they may adopted a particularly negative mode/style of interacting with others; which may be due to other events that have occurred in their life -not mention above; such as a particular learned negative conditioning experience(s); that may cause them to adapt their particular mode of behavior (blaming other); which may generalized itself into their every day waking life (as they interact with others)." [7]

Their particular mode of interacting may also manifest itself in verbal an or physical behavior (abuse)."Some actors are just

---

Valley, California.

[6] Satir, Virginia., (9-6-2016) 5 Satir Categories For Understanding Communication Styles (Sources of insight.Com) Book Nuggets

[7] Allen, W . (1981), The effects of operant control on disruptive behavior doing swimming instructions, University of Wisconsin/Publications-Milwaukee, Wisconsin.

ncorrigible; as they project blame/responsibility on others; an some do not want to hear any exclamation(s) that explains their behavior(s); as they feel more comfortable in their system of functioning –literally in the dark of negative thinking." [8]

"Once you literally attempt to exposed their 'dark dysfunctional system(s)' of; how they frequently attempt to blame others as they interact with them; to the light of positive thinking; they become very defensive (cycling through various modes of communicating an various defense mechanisms); shrinking back into the comfort of the darkness of negative thinking; where they may function at that or similar level(s) (mention above) and feel some measure of comfortable."

"At this point it may be of interest to note, that some research seem to suggest, the probability of actors who appear to be "literally frequent chronic complainers, have a low probability of changing how they interact with others." "As such they generally cognitively (literally) view others as the blame/cause of their problems/situations they find themselves in – irrespective of their own related actions or a lack there of."

Your nemesis/the other person you're in a relationship with may need therapy or worse yet; possibly you may need therapy too; particularly; if it was an emotionally bruising debilitating situation/relationship. "Or, of your own free will you elect to remain in the relationship; then the both of you are/maybe candidates for therapy (individual or couple as the case may be)." [9] The later is further qualified by the need of the involvement of

[8] Allen,W .(2012) Scared affair, Xlbris/Publications, Indianapolis, Indiana.

[9] Allen,W .(Comments), (1996)W hatMen Find Sexy, (Upscale Communications Inc)Atlanta,Ga.
   P 34.

competent professional(s) in such matters; involving a plan for safety first, assessments, treatment plans, treatments recommendations, referrals, an other interventions related to a desirable outcome or dissolution.

The "plane" on which they operate upon is limited. But ironically can literally cover vast emotional distances! This mental or emotional mode of functioning maybe on a subconscious level "As a result they may not be aware of the harm they can cause others; that it's always someone else's fault; say namely you are the target now; as they have conditioned you an feel comfortable/confident you may respond in particular way(s); resulting in you becoming their convenient an reliable target of focus; an as a result they may now operate upon you with impunity."

While there may not be many direct links of research correlating with "the effects of negative personalities on the functioning of others" per/se; I'm convinced that the phenomenon is significant an exit on a highly unknown but quantifiable level. It maybe described as a personality who is insecure, inadequate, and otherwise do not think or regard themselves very highly -respectively. It attempts to manipulate an otherwise control others, as they interact with them invoking emotional Responses, such as feeling of guilt, lack of confidence, fault, blame, etc. They may further literally try/insist on "prior authorizations;" characterized by having their approval/control on any actions you may "think or dream" of taking; before you may proceed on any "independent" task/actions of your own." A clue For future reference that you did not ask for their permission; is just one example exemplified in the following sentence! "Well you didn't tell me you were going to call the office today (etcetera)." The desired response as they attempt to minimize an control you is to cause you to experience feelings of the "pain of guilt;" for not asking or letting them know you were going to call the office; thereby motivating you to ask for their permission in the future). This may have a generalizing effect! It may subconsciously motivate you to ask for permission on most endeavors.

Chapter Four/Get help

In order to protect Yourself from the debilitating effects of the negative influences of being involved in such a relationship(s); consider your safety first; otherwise, you must at least come to realize that you are in such a relationship; an in general try to understand how the dynamics of such a negative symbiotic relationship May works. [10]

In an attempt to extricate one's self from such a broken system, the question becomes, "can it be fixed, cured, saved, salvaged, etcetera?"

In an attempt to extricate one's self from such a Broken system;the helpful truth may lie in the fact that everything cannot be "fixed;" and out of indifference; some will still not choose to do so.

"If you stayed too long in the darkness of a negative unproductive symbiotic relationship; in circumstances characterized by, verbal violence, physical domestic violence, economics challenges, fear of estrangement; or just the idea of

---

[10]Allen,W . (1981),The effects of operant control on disruptive behavior doing sw im m ing instructions,University of W isconsin/Publications—M ilw aukee,W isconsin.

going your separate way(s), facing the daily challenges (unknowns) of life; may not be an encouraging incentive(s) to leave." "But, in some situations it may just be up to you to ferret out your concerns, an safely extricate yourself from such a relationship." "Or you can passively rely on others to rescue you; which maybe to late or never arrives."

"Some of the key dynamics to look for are, the use of blame, control, injected condescending acts, and remarks that leave you in doubt of your self. As a result you may experience feelings of being forlorn, a lack of confidence, a haunting feeling you may have forgotten something, that it's your fault, and you maybe inadequate in future undertakings i.e., self improvement, enlightenment, future aspirations/goals, as well as challenges of daily living."

Other dynamics used by an actor maybe the use of illusion and suggestion; when it may help to attain their objectives. Remember, an illusion (visible/audible or not can be used as a means to deceive) can have an emotional effect. Suggestions (to conjure up an image or idea) depending on how employed can have emotional effects too. Their use (particularly when used subliminally) can be very effective; as they may enhance the goals of the actor; as they employ various approaches/techniques in conjunction with the "blamer mode." "Although, there are several different modes people communicate in; the blamer mode is usually preferred by an actor; as it is usually effective an maybe 'convenient ' to adaptively used when experiencing stress, anxiety, decomposition, etc; as it seems to help decrease their stress an may help to acquire desired results (particular responses from you)."

A relationship forged with the use of blame is secondary only to the non productive defense mechanism of suspicion; upon which neither can be employed for a foundation to build a positive productive relationship(s). [11] With this in mind it would further appear the probability of an actor changing his behavior remains very low; as they also may see themselves as "not" the blame in any way; for anything an furthermore do not need or desire to change. However, to be fair there may be some exceptions...

If one is unknowingly being victimized, " their perception of the status of their relationship maybe froth with faulty logic!" They may respond in such away that is consistent with their state of mind; as the effects of blame continues thereby powering the dynamics that help spawn an unhealthy cycling symbiotic relationship. They may even experience momentary somatic or other concerns that are not articulated here; but the resulting functionality is the same; an can further contribute to the persistence of such a hurtful cycling relationship.

"Because actor(s) may have personality flaws, no confidence in themselves, etcetera ; they may not feel important (appreciated) and that you are of the same opinion." Subsequently, they feel inadequate and attempt to compensate themselves, by controlling you by some means (as they interact with you), such as blame, fear, doubt, etc.

For example blaming you an declaring they are not at fault, thereby making themselves feel whole/compensated (For the moment) and you feeling guilty. This is just another example

---

[11]Allen W . (1962) Social Science VS Racial Prejudice, Milwaukee Journal/Publications, Milwaukee, Wisconsin.

15

of another dynamic of the relationship that aids in maintains its momentum.

The end result is you may not consciously realize, how/why you are experience feelings of uneasiness, blame. Etc. But, it may not be your fault. However, you would think "deep down inside" one instinctively realizes this! However, Sometimes we may need to hear if for someone else; less we may continue to think we are the cause (fault) of the "dysfunction" in the relationship; an as a result may need help in the process of extricating one's self from the offending person/situation/relationship/etcetera.

With this in mind one of the keys maybe, learning How to validate yourself (resolve unresolved conflicts, come to terms with them, an put them behind you). Get to know who you are, that you are of value, an you have dignity an self worth. Decide what you want out of life as well as how you want to be treated. [12] "The quality of how you want to be treated is important."

Don't wait for answers to come from unreliable sources; as they may respectively produce undesirable negative results. If you are depending on the wrong person(s) help, you may be predictably in for a continuous menu of self doubt, feelings of guilt, and injections of blame, etc. If you attempt to use information from an unreliable source, the Undesired end result(s) may be the lack of attainment IE., failure, limited functioning, never attaining your desires, secret aspirations, potential, goals, or even a long needed vacation, etc. The Repeated injections of blame will continues.

I repeat you must also come to realize; they blame everyone else for their problems (not themselves). "Subsequently, they can't

[12] Jones, Dasha, (1996   ), W hatM en Find Sexy, (Upscale Com m unications Inc), Atlanta, Ga. P 34.

blame themselves because you an others are the cause." "Even if they admit to blame, they may interact appropriately, an it would only be momentary at best."

Also try to realize the reality of relationships is that they may progress through stages i.e., beginning, interim, and what's revealed/develops during those times may determine the outcome (should it continues, make adjustments, or consider termination). "For example relations that lead to marriage, or other forms of unions may usually involve stages such as initial awareness of the individual, information about the same, physical attraction, courting, exploring potential areas of compatibility, etcetera, and as time goes by, it is either dissolved or continues in some form or another (an estranged or otherwise)."

The lesson being relations may not last for what ever reason; as such be forewarned to attempt to prepare yourself in the event the outcome is not positive. "There are many areas of preparation, such as your mental an physical health; as well as financial, support, backup plans, etcetera; in an attempt to prepare for what ever the future outcome may be." " The phenomena of waiting for 'Mr. or Miss. right' as well as 'Mr. or Miss. nice person' may not likely be reliable." [13] It is just as ridiculous as trying to keep up with the Jones; as they do not exist either; as it is a creation of illusion; which seem to suggest it is not wise to enter into a relationship for the sake of it. Be mindful relationships transcend stages! Observe how they handle stress and solve problems . It would also be helpful if you could obtain any mental health information (if possible from parents, friends, or maybe a computer searches if indicated, etc.), "Just I love you is not enough."

---

[13] Allen,W .(2012) Scared affair, Xlibris/Publications, Indianapolis, Indiana.

It is wise to have a plan if you anticipate involvement in a relationship. If it is a domestic relationship that doesn't work out, you should have other alternatives! For example it can be as simple as, "arranging with your parents to have your bedroom available in the event you have to move back home." There are variations of such planning. The objective being is to have a safe alternative to return/retreat to (as in plan A or B). It could be as simple as a planed stay with parents relatives, friends, etc., as there are at least several ways to arrange such. [14]

Finally, if you find your self in a similar situation; it may ultimately be up to you to safely initiate some action to bring it to a safe resolution. In some instances there may not be an agreeable resolution! They may not be willing or won't go quietly. "Depending on their behavior; help may be indicated at this point."

"As the recipient or with the help of others (where indicated) must determine if the relationship is toxic; and may not be for you under any circumstances –and abandon it." If your safety is at risk it must be done diplomatically -as possible. If indicated some how you must literally muster up enough emotional/psychic strength to pursue the appropriate course of action. You may contemplate, if there is no threat to your safety, should I throw them out or just leave. Either scenario may be dangerous. They may not Be willing to go quietly. You may even need protection (If you can't do it safely).

"If indicated, Consider Professional help in such matters!"

[14] Allen W . (1962) Social Science VS Racial Prejudice, Milwaukee Journal/Publications, Milwaukee, Wisconsin.

That may range from a consultation with a police department, or the services of other professionals, who are experts in such matters. "A court order may be indicated contingent upon the circumstances!" "They may not be willing to go quietly." At that point depending on their behavior (emotional, verbal, or physical abuse) help may be clearly indicated.

Be truthful to yourself! "If you feel emotionally exhausted (feel weak, drained, feel trapped, need help); or just to afraid and confused an feel you do not know what to do; whatever your emotive status may be; perhaps you can acquire the help of a mental health professional; who may help you assess the situation." "After an assessment based on the urgency of the situation, histories, clinical interviews, tests, psychosocial data base, etcetera; they may suggest specific actions, treatments an possibly referrals to further assist you; as your career, your precious sleep, aspirations, or safety/life maybe in the balance." It can also have an effect on your business/job, as well as personal affairs with relatives an others. Even with professional help or that of others the outcome may depend on how you react to address the issues. You might want to ask yourself, "do you want to spend a life time in a nonproductive negative situation, and otherwise during the natural course of life events literally die unhappy?"

If Indicted, domestic violence brought to the courts attention can often help resolve such relationships issues; if nothing else, a no contact order may resolve the issues of safety. Sometimes the help of protective sworn officers/ authorities are indicated. They may even work in tandem with professional civilian organizations specializing in protecting victims in such matters.

Chapter Five/Conclusion and recommendations

"The purpose of the above aforegoing is to explain an recognize the difference between experiencing symptoms of a temporary EM (not at a clinical level such as depression, etcetera); that may remit with an explanation(s) of its dynamics, etcetera." "Or are you experiencing a more disturbing manifestation of the symptoms of an EM; that may be toxic (may be at a clinical level); which maybe secondary to a particular type of relationship; where as the EM continue to manifest its self in disturbances of emotional feelings of being inadequate; an as a result professional services maybe indicated." "As a result you maybe unhappy or just depressed; an for some unexplainable reason; you may not be consciously aware of; you are not able to reach a particular(s) level of attainment (challenges of daily living, goals, potentials, etcetera)."

We examine the characteristics of such individuals an how to possibly protect yourself from the ravages of being involved in such a relationship(s).

We further delineated upon the functioning of such a personality; which may suggest ideas of what to look for when trying to discern if there is a potential for a desirable (equitable) relationship.

Finally, if you are currently in such a relationship; or anticipate involvement; there are many options to explored; with regards to how to protect yourself from potential adversities.

"EM could exist when you allow someone to effect you emotionally in such away, that you are unable to attain your real or perceived potential as well as other desires."

"The emotional malaise syndrome may not necessarily occur in a personal relation; depending on the circumstances; it may occur in relationships with parent(s), friends colleagues, supervisors, etc." It could occur in incidental/situational relationship(s); that maybe more transitory in nature.

Try to Learn to become more adept at recognizing their modus operand(s). Try to learn to recognize the Characteristics an methods, as once they feel confident, secure, an invested in the relationship, they may proceed to effect you in emotionally painful ways aforementioned…

The truth maybe your response/reaction could be w/ in the norm! But, you may think something is wrong with your reaction. However, upon further examination it is revealed you may not be the total cause of the paradox.

The "cause" may lie within your relationship with say your significant other (actor), who interacts with you (recipient) in such a way, as to make you feel, think, and act as you do.

At the risk of being repetitive, once again the following is being brought to awareness! The phenomena may also occurred in informal, infrequent, non intimate relationships as well! They may also have an effect upon how you react too! For example some how you feel its your fault things are not going as you think they should; an your response may be similar to a failing intimate relationship; once again exhibiting core dynamics of a malfunctioning relationship; while the actor exhibit the other(s). It is wise to remember none intimate relationships are usually transitory in nature; if possible take care they do not take on characteristics of a malfunctioning significant intimate relationship(s)."

"When it inadvertently effect your daily functioning; in activities of daily living or emotionally to the point you are unable to reach or approximate your desired potential or goals, real, imaginary, perceived, or otherwise; it may usually be defined as a problem when it interferes with your everyday functioning in such a way; that you are not functioning normally; or as you would like or intended to; considering your actual capabilities that appear to be depressed at that time; at this point one might respectively reflect upon,

"well now you know."

"What choices will you make?"

"No matter what is said, one may further surmise some people /couples, just do not belong together!" "In a society that promotes togetherness via a culture of institutions, friendships, clubs, secret organizations, ceremonies, marriage, etcetera; bound by your word an their expectations; it's sometimes difficult to transition out of relationships due to their influences, expectations, sanctions, etcetera, it may have on you an others)." "Even without these influences, it is important to note how important your personnel expectations of a relationship are to you; as it is up to you; an if all else fails you must make that decision to get help if indicated. "Moving forward in that direction, also keeping in mind, how you achieve what you accomplish is just as important as your objectives!" "Or in other words how you go about it can increase or decrease the risk of physical harm to yourself or others, as some actors have difficulty accepting change.." In emergency situations intervention via 911 (as well as other optional resources it may trigger) may be required. This is a determination to be made if diplomacy an other efforts fails; you or someone must decide if the use of such resources are indicated."

"Also keep in mind there are approximately five or more identifiable modes that people can electively use to communicate with to others.. The one of primary concern here is the blamer mode; which does not preclude the actor from using other modes of communication; that may be convenient to further obtain their objective(s). "Initially, while under stress it is possible they may adapt this mode of communicating; as they become more comfortable/fluent in it; as it serves their purposes (reducing stress and possibly as an unintended consequence coincidentally learn to controlling you/others); which may generalize into their everyday mode of interaction with others; and may become a style or a way of communicating (specifically those they target)."

"There is no attempt here to be satirical; but you must learn how to validate yourself; an become more comfortable an confident in yourself."

Stay out of the darkness of negative thinking too! "Try to Know who you are; what you want and what you are willing to compromise, etcetera." Also consider, "what direction your moral compass may points as well as your dignity." "This span of time (you occupy) referred to as life is to short; to allow yourself to be continuously injected (with negative verbal/physical abusive behavior -etcetera) by an actor employing these alternatives; causing you to feel/thinking you are living under a cloud of intimation as well as it's all your fault too."

"If, after becoming aware of this phenomena and you allow the process to persist in its wake –allowing it to continue to effect you; it would seem it is not acceptable as you must 'become' to know, believe; and otherwise realize you are (uniquely one of a kind) one of the many most profound miracles that has ever occurred throught this universe!" "With it comes a potentially unique ability to modify/change your environment." "But, yet you may literally allow these verbal behavioral suggestions an illusions to minimize and otherwise render you to an unacceptable position in your relationship(s)." "The irony maybe that the individual who is acting upon you may not be consciously aware of the purpose of their behavior or the resulting effect/impact/outcome it has upon you."

"The actor may not be consciously aware of acting in this manner, as the success of the use of such behavioral interactions in the past, that may have long since been forgotten, is habitually used to help them acquire/attain desirable ends, and as a result have reinforced/encouraged the use of that behavior."

Try to utilize some guidelines/moral values, how you want to be treated, excreta; that you may bring from your prior life experience(s); that you can set for yourself before seeking a relationship(s). "One example could be how you want to be treated, as you interact with others in a relationship."

How to protect yourself:

It may be a difficult challenge to protect yourself as you must try to be prepared, mentally, emotionally, financially, etcetera ; even if you are flexible in your approach; try to get it right as possible the first time or continue your search when indicated; as the best of intentions may result in unintended consequences. "There just may not be a Mr., Mrs., or Ms. right either; an perhaps you shouldn't wait for someone on a white horse; coming alone (either) to literally sweeping you off your feet; leading you to think that they appear to have the desirable qualities you seek."

"Furthermore, before consider entering into a relationship, you may need to come to terms with realizing some aspects of your life, which you respond to, are just illusions, often times coupled with suggestions."

"For example trying to keep up with the Joneses (who are not real)! But, we try anyway even through we have consciously long since forgotten; our longings an desires may have been motivated by unseen subliminal powers; such as the projected illusions of fashions; and their equally powerful suggestive advertisements in various medias."

"With the aforegoing in mind friends/others may appear to be in ideal happy relationships; but it just may be an illusion an or suggestion of the same; suggest that one should not enter into relationships based on appearance, suggestion, etcetera. Needless to say where appropriate, when contemplating entering into a relationship, it should be for the right reasons."

"The power of suggestion" is very awesome/potent! You need to know/realize people are not necessarily who or what they "appear" to be. The way they may appear (initially) an interact with you may literally be nothing more than a mask; disguising who they really are (their personality as well as their intentions); or it could be a preview of the consequences of becoming involved in a relationship with them, etcetera." Personality generally refers to how one usually respond, act ,or behave as they attempt to solve the range of daily challenges of life (including stress). There are more comprehensive definitions. The pathology of how one arrives at becoming a particular personality is as varied as there are people. "Some explanations are their experiences as they grow up." Another explanation is the foundation of personality is set at an early age. [15] Some of their experiences could be related to poor parenting skills, the quality of interaction with others during formative years, bonding, physical/verbal abuse, mental illness, emotional problems, bullying, an a litany of other reasons –to be sure. Other reasons may be congenital or neurological. Don't forget the potential or limitation of their own abilities. Anyone of these reasons (or others) can manifest itself in their behavior; as they interact with others; if the desired results are reinforced; that particular behavior will most likely repeatedly/frequently be used (habit). [16]

"Even the way one talks can be use as a mask to disguise/hiding the true occupant within, the mind, the indwelling personality; as they initially pretend to function within normal limits; an at

[15]Alport,Gordon (1937)W hat it the Trait Theory of Personality, updated by Kendra,cherry Aug 2–6-2016 at verywell.com /trait theory on personality 2795955

[16]Allen,W . (1981),The effects of operant control on disruptive behavior doing sw im m ing instructions,University of W isconsin/Publications–M ilw aukee,W isconsin.

opportune times via verbal behavior emotionally injecting into a naïve unsuspecting victim feelings of blame, guilt, or fault; thereby setting them up for a relationship based upon a disguise and thereby lead to an undesirable outcome ." The actor's benefits can be relief from stressors that manifest themselves emotional mental, somatic, etcetera. This behavior may also help the actor to compensate for their own "feelings of Inadequacies." Keep in mind change maybe difficult for such an actor (regardless of their reason or rational). Their behavior may also be related to a particular conditioning experience: neurological problems, physical and or emotional trauma, etc. They may just choose to function the way they do; even through they have the capacity to change; or to be that way for no particular reason other than they "feel like it." "They may not appreciate who they are, an choose from many Sub cultural Styles to function in, as they present themselves in a particular way." "They may just want to imitate or pretend to be someone other than who they are; or they may not want to change how they interact with others (as simple or complicated as that).

Before getting into a relationship a wise and sage one would advise, "the first thing you do before getting evolve in a relationship is have an alternative plan (in the event it does work out)."

"That is ridiculous," a new lover may say.

"We are soul mates."

"We were meant for each other."

Or, "We belong together!" Possible suggesting entering into an exclusive relation; which is usually consummated before either party know much of the information mention above (about what one should attempt to know about an individual before entering into a particular relationship).

But, a wise old Sage one may say, "perhaps you had better slow down! It may not last. Having a plan is not a bad idea."

Some plan(s) may be as simple as, " mom don't change or rent my room in the event and intended relationship does not work out."

Be honest an explain, "you don't want to be inadvertently trapped in a relationship, where indications are you shouldn't be in." It would also be wise to have reserve finances (so called mad money) in the event you have to leave a situation/relationship.

You can further protect yourself by getting to know yourself an try to answer, "who am I?" " If you don't; learn to like who you are an become your best advocate -not your worst enemy." Also try to answer, "is this what I really want?" "In the meantime learn as much as you can about the functioning of the personality of the intended one i.e., how they solve problems, how they defend themselves (an what about), self reports/assessments, their family history, how do they responded to anxiety, stress, daily challenges of life, what activities they participated in at school, and if they had any friends. You may also consider how long the relationships lasted, how were issues resolved as they arose, an how they functioned at work, school, an play)." "Nevertheless, no matter what is disclosed, you see, hear, or believe; always have a plan in the event it does not work out. The list above is by no means conclusive. It suggest areas of the individual's functioning you may want to inquire into; as you attempt to make an assessment; an no matter what aspects of a person's life is examined; there are always quirks (as you may miss something obvious or unseen)." You may find yourself mauling over, "what if I would have, should have, or could have." Nevertheless Sometimes hard choices have to be made (to hold on or let go) If you feel unable or unwilling to make such a determination; as an adjunct talking with friends, pastor, parents, siblings, etcetera or professionals may be indicated.

Otherwise, "the alternative maybe comparable to serving a long prison sentence of a life time w/ someone you should not be with; at your own emotional and cognitive expense; an perhaps with haunting ruminating underlying thoughts of; why am I experiencing these feeling of fault, blame, dread, guilt, doubt, etcetera?" "Although, it may not necessarily be your fault; other than you have not consciously (inadvertently/unknowingly) allowed this particular manifestation(s) of the emotional malaise syndrome (EMS) to persist in your life to your own determent."

EMS is commonly experienced as it can happen to anyone; as countless millions suffer needlessly in such relations; but, it does not necessarily mean you are mentally sick or in need of treatment. "However, if it is indicated; then professional intervention may be needed." "Never forget it's your life!" "It belongs to you." "What happens next maybe contingent upon you."

If what you Desire/seek to attain is not accomplished during a particular period of an apparently troubled relationship; it maybe concluded that it should be ended; an if not then what are the options? There are many! "Ideally, it would appear, when relationships approach a point when they maybe dissolve, keep in mind there maybe some difficulty during those times involving Contingencies, reconciliation, resistance, potentials thereof, etcetera."

"During those time(s) you may consider if you (with the help of a professional, etcetera) deem any of those options safe an reasonable; which may or not seem unreasonable; that you (including the actor) may want to attempt to preserve the relationship; once there is an understanding of what the dynamics of the problems are; an there is a potential for positive change an it is further deemed to be a safe an reasonable option."

"It would seem such a proposal would involve endeavoring to communicate honestly with each other; with a standing agreement (involving continuous learning in that particular) to be able to "agree" to disagree; without hurting or injuring each other verbally, Physically, or emotionally; as well as via none verbal/physical/emotional means such as decreasing an controlling active or passive aggressive behavior, etcetera."

"Instead, rather strive for a fluid transparent relationship; whereby you can communication freely (exchanging ideas/issues/beliefs/concern regarding one's welfare, etcetera); about their dilemmas in the relationship as well as other pertinent matters; and not desire or attempt to destroy each other emotionally, physically, financially, etcetera."

"Critically. if the above is not feasible (considering your safety first); It would not seem unreasonable, that you in particular, have a Personnel responsibility (to save yourself), to make an assessment with the help of a competent professional, etcetera - if needed, for assistance to assess which course(s) of action you may consider taking such as, involving your safety (first), protection, remediation, counseling, or otherwise means of extricating yourself from what may often times could be characterized as a life (term) involving a hurtful unsocialized /uncivilized "emotional relationship(s)." "Furthermore, with that in mind do not complicate the issues by being unforgiving, seeking revenge, or otherwise impune any forward progress; as the issues may become long term; thereby leaving an opportunity for the actor to attempt to renew the undesirable relationship; 'or worst' being unforgiving an revengeful may make healing in the matter even more difficult."

If indicated it maybe best to be "done" with the relationship. There maybe legal matters, financial matters, property, minor children, excreta involved. If the actor is an opportunist it may be best to resolve these legal matters with dispatch in court, ie., as they can issue specific orders regarding, safety, financial matters, supervision, support, as well as schedules of visitation where minor children are involved. "Otherwise, emotionally the relationship may never end! "As it can be further complicated where minors are involved, as they may require both parties to communicate regarding their health, wellbeing, education, legal matters, written permission for various activities, an a host of other unforeseen difficulties -that may arise requiring the attention of both parties (ie., particularly for example if it involves the health an education of minor(s) who are issues of the relationship)."

You can further learn to protect yourself by being emotionally an financially prepared (by having your own an not depend on the gratitude of others); as well as not depending on magical thinking, good luck, gambling, wishes, superstition, or promises, etcetera. "Some of these alternatives may not be reliable -putting it mildly." "Be prepared by planning your own means in life to support decisions you anticipate making; as it is never a good idea to depend on others for the same." "That being said and understood;if the relationship does not work out; You may not be trapped there in possibly a hostile environment due to poor financial preparedness an it's consequences."

Furthermore, other signs and symptoms to look for may include remembering, that they may make very subtle use of "guilt!" "They are quite adapt at it; be it on a conscious level or not." They are quite proficient at emotionally injecting feelings of guilt into the cognition of others. "You may not be aware of the process you are being set up for!" "Once you're are literally emotionally infected; start feeling guilty; an being a person of your word; has kept many together in untenable relationships than should not exist."

The person who's behavior (Verbal, physical, etcetera) causing you so much grief may not think any thing is wrong with their activities; let alone errant enough to warrant a DSM diagnosis or any other label. Nevertheless, you may not belong together. It may be as simple or Complex as that! "A mismatch?" "If so, consider an alternative to your relationship (with the help of a competent professional or others of your choice)." "Furthermore," be aware not to be literally guided (influenced) by such clichés as; "until death do we part," "we were made for each other," "we are soul mates," "etcetera!" "Less the question then maybe come; depending on your response; how can we be apart; thereby possibly setting one up for a revisit/return to a failed relationship."

They may further state, "there must be something I/we are not doing; which can be factored into the until death do we part (etcetera) kind of intriguing statements/thinking/mentality.' "Furthermore, the literally binding rules of instutions, secret societies, sanctions, ceremonies, contemporary thinking superstition, promises of others (that are transmitted culturally an internalized), must be examined (in relationship to some circumstances involved in relationships), as they may inadvertently energize the cycle of the dynamics of the functioning of some malfunctioning relationships, that may cause you to be in 'harms way', as well as holding you back physically, emotionally, financially, impune your confidence, that may otherwise, impede/obstruct/prevents you from true growth as an individual, an otherwise prevent the essence of the fulfillment of your, dreams, goals, desires, aspirations, potential abilities, etcetera, from blossoming into fruitation."